ISBN-10: 1530429900

Swear Word Adult Coloring Book

Stress Relief Coloring Book
with Sweary Words, Animals and Flowers

To: _____

From: _____

unibulpress.com

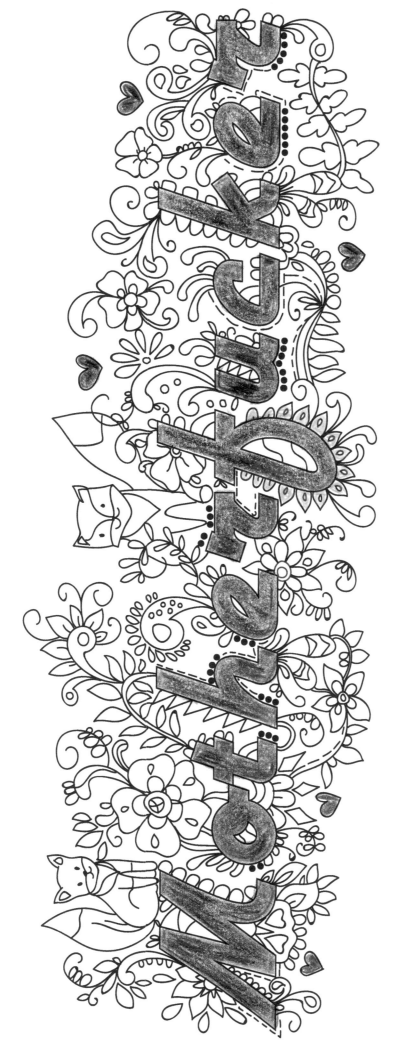

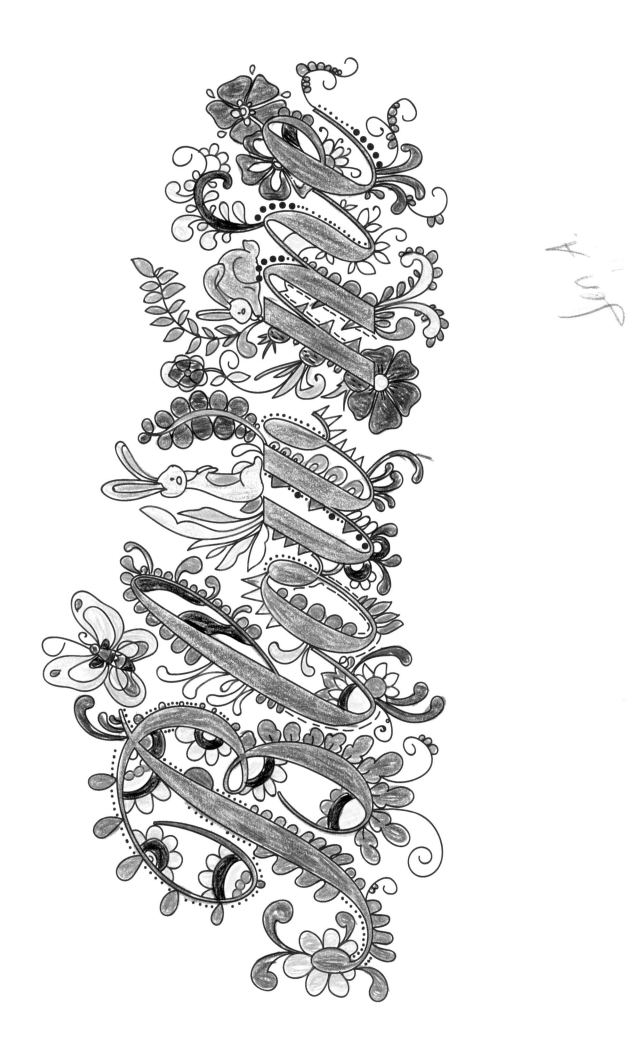

Palette Test Sheet

Thank You!

We want to thank you for purchasing this book!
If you enjoyed this book, then I'd like to ask you for a favor,
would you be kind enough to leave a review for this book
on Amazon? It'd be greatly appreciated!

Make sure you follow us:
facebook.com/adultcoloringpress/
instagram.com/unibulpress/
pinterest.com/unibulpress/

unibulpress.com

If you have colored a page from our book and upload it
to any social media please make sure you tag us or link to
the book.

Thank you again for purchasing!